T5-CUU-949

Teaching and Learning with EARLY ELEMENTARY CHILDREN

A Manual for Workers in the Church

Muriel E. Lichtenwalner and Arline J. Ban

Illustrations by Linda Weller

Judson Press ® Valley Forge

TEACHING AND LEARNING WITH EARLY ELEMENTARY CHILDREN

Copyright © 1979
Judson Press, Valley Forge, PA 19482-0851

Second Printing, 1984

All rights reserved. No part of this publication may be reproduced, stored in a retrieval system, or transmitted in any form or by any means, electronic, mechanical, photocopying, recording, or otherwise, without the prior permission of the copyright owner, except for brief quotations included in a review of the book.

Library of Congress Cataloging in Publication Data
Lichtenwalner, Muriel E., and Ban, Arline J.
  Teaching and learning with early elementary children.

  Bibliography: p. 62
  Includes index.
  1. Elementary School teaching. I. Title.
LB1555.L6   372.1'1'02   78-25955
ISBN 0-8170-0802-0

The name JUDSON PRESS is registered as a trademark in the U.S. Patent Office.
Printed in the U.S.A. ⊕

Contents

Introduction

Welcome to a special group—workers with children in the church! What challenged you to teach? Do you teach because you feel, "Well, it *is* my turn and someone has to do it!"? Or do you teach because you can say, "I really like those children! It will be fun working with them!"? Perhaps you remember people who helped you in your early growing years! Now you feel, "I can share my faith!" Whatever your reason, you know that working with children in the fellowship of the church is unique!

Working with children in the church is more than teaching a lesson! It is:

- sharing experiences with children,
  - taking time to discover children as persons,
    - observing and listening to the ways God moves in the lives of children.

You are invited to read this book to discover new ways to understand the children with whom you minister and new possibilities for creative teaching.

1

Who Are They?

Here they come: the children you are teaching. They're alike in some ways, but so different in others.

There's Manuel, who is absolutely full of it! Most of your boys and girls are active and on the go, but Manuel is something else.

Sally is a careful little worker. Everything has to be just right or she isn't satisfied with herself. She becomes very upset if she gets paint or paste on her clothing.

Here comes Maria, a real question box. "What's this for?" "Why are we going to do that?" Most of the children are curious, but Maria seems to have a built-in question mark in her brain. She's a real joy to teach and she keeps you on the alert thinking up answers. But sometimes . . . !

Here's TV Chuck! He must spend most of his time at home in front of the television set. Last year he rode an imaginary motorcycle to class each week. I wonder who his favorite TV character will be this year?

Now there's Jill, who requires extra love and attention because her mother is in the hospital. Be careful, though; the other children in the class will be quick to notice if you make a pet of her.

You will have to step lively to keep up with José! He is always the first one to finish his work; and unless you manage to keep him busy, he'll find his own amusement.

It may be a mistake to try to describe the characteristics of an age group; each child is an individual with a unique personality, set of interests, and range of abilities. But every teacher needs to have some idea of what to expect of a group of children. All children of a particular grade level will not be comparable in ability or in achievement. Some school systems introduce the teaching of basic skills earlier than others, and the growing trend is to teach several levels in one classroom, allowing the children to progress at their own speed.

Some first graders will be able to read at third grade level, while others will be able to do little more than recognize their own names in print. Some first graders will have better control of their emotions than some children in third grade.

The purpose of this section is to introduce you to children of the early elementary age (grades one through three, usually ages six through eight) and to provide a range of their characteristics. How this information relates to Christian education will be discussed in a later section.

The road toward independence begins a little earlier for children today than it did for many who are adults now. Many first graders have attended kindergarten, and some will have had the advantage of nursery school. For these children, first grade isn't quite the period of change and adjustment that it is for those who are just stepping out of the world of home and family. It still is a time of transition, though, as they face increasing opportunities in an ever-widening world.

Physical Growth

An abundance of energy and the continuing growth of large muscles make it difficult for early elementary children to sit still for a very long period of time. Even when they are sitting, they seem to be in constant motion, squirming from side to side and swinging their legs. Hopping, skipping, jumping, and running are among their favorite activities!

Gradually the small muscles develop, permitting more skillful use of the hands and eye-hand coordination. Painting, pasting, and construction activities become neater, and children take more pride in their work as they mature.

Compared to previous stages, the tempo of constructive activity increases; the children want to get things done and are impatient when there are delays.

Emotional Development

Emotionally, early elementary children are going through significant changes. They are experiencing new feelings and new action patterns, going quickly from smiles to tears and from love to anger. They want to be grown-up, but act in immature ways; they want to be independent, but don't know how; they find it hard to make decisions because they want everything "most." They need physical contact with each other and with their teachers. They want the undivided and immediate attention of the teacher when something important pops into their heads.

Gradually they become increasingly aware of the others in their world and are more sensitive to approval or disapproval of other persons, adults in particular. Although early elementary children see parents as models for behavior, they also choose heroes and heroines from television shows or books; these are the characters they will imitate.

They are eager to try things out and discover what their world is all about. Often they are frustrated by the lack of physical ability to do the things they really want to do.

Most young children are not afraid of or ashamed of showing affection. They need to feel loved and wanted. A sense of trust within the family is important. They like to be entrusted with responsibilities. The same type of trust, however, may not be extended to outsiders. Sometimes mistrust has been taught in the home as a means of survival in a cruel world.

Social Development

Young children are not self-conscious with each other or with teachers and other adults. Actually they can be very frank. One teacher reported that a new child in her class greeted her with, "My, but you're fat!" Early elementary children tease each other, but they are quick to offer comfort to one who has suffered physically or mentally.

They are ready at this point for group activities and realize that it is necessary to win the approval of other boys and girls. However, they often go about this in ways which do not produce the desired results. They need a great deal of help in determining how to be fair and unselfish.

Increasingly they try hard to be on an equal basis with their age mates. Winning at games and success in activities are very important. They are beginning now to develop ideas of what is good and what is bad. They want to be good, but often fail in their efforts. This failure may lead to making alibis and putting the blame on others.

It becomes more and more important to belong. Boys and girls tend to stay in separate groups, for they are becoming more conscious of sexual differences. After a period of time and participation in a uniting group activity, they will work and play together.

Early elementary children may be sticklers for rules and inclined to be bossy, especially when they are with younger children. With guidance, however, they can be good helpers with younger boys and girls.

Success and expressions of appreciation from others are important for self-esteem. Failures, even small ones, can hurt.

Intellectual Development

Beginning in the early stages of childhood, boys and girls try to make sense out of the world. But they will be well past the third grade before they can reason and understand cause and effect.

School offers them the opportunity to acquire certain skills in reading, writing, and mathematics which will add to their powers of observing, experimenting, and analyzing. Through many and varied experiences children become able to generalize and think abstractly. From birth through third grade, they are still thinking in "bits and pieces." Most children are eager to learn, but the early elementary child has an interest span usually of not more than fifteen minutes. Children at this stage have a poor concept of time. They are fascinated with things they can feel and smell, and they are curious about everything they see and hear. In other words, they think concretely, rather than abstractly.

Since they are learning to read and print capital and small letters, any charts and signs which they are expected to read should be printed this way.

As children continue to learn, language development is rapid and words become tools which they are able to use rather well. Then they begin to ask questions, thus adding to their fund of information. Their questions become thoughtful, and some of their ideas are quite amazing.

"Why do we thank God for everything, when some things are bad?" asked one seven-year-old.

"I would really like to know why Jesus had to die. It seems to me he could have done more good living," commented an eight-year-old.

"How would you like somebody kicking dirt in your hole?" asked a third grader indignantly when another child began pushing dirt into a hole leading to the home of a field mouse.

Even though many children are able to read material meant for their grade level, they still like to listen to stories. (Stories meant for hearing are often more interesting than those the children can read.) They have a larger listening vocabulary than a reading vocabulary.

By using their gifts of imagination, they are able to think of different things to do and different ways to carry out projects. But for many it is easier to fall into a pattern than to "do their own thing." A third grade teacher has commented that our culture encourages persons to meet only the minimum requirements.

Children of this age enjoy what some might call nonsense—word plays and clowning—and they giggle readily.

While they respond eagerly to most suggestions, they make it clear that they have minds of their own, too. With some exceptions, they are far more interested in exploring and discovering new things than they are in following directions for formal games and crafts. They dearly love adventure.

Environmental Influences

Children take their environmental influences and past experiences with them wherever they go. Just as there is no "average" child, there is no "average" environment, either. Love and the sense of being important to someone are vital to the growth and development of a child. These are found as readily in an inner-city apartment as in a suburban split-level home.

What particular strengths and needs do children from varying backgrounds often bring with them?

The viewpoints which children of a rural environment can offer a church school group differ from those of suburban area children. For instance, the child (referred to earlier) who pushed dirt into the hole leading to the home of a field mouse came from a farm. He later explained to the teacher and other children that mice damage the crops. A farmer's child knows many things about animals, growing food supplies, and natural resources which can be shared with other children. Rural children may have more opportunities to be with their families since life is centered on the farm. They probably will have specific responsibilities, and the family will work together.

Inner-city children learn a sense of responsibility and acquire a degree of independence very early in life. When parents and other adults in the family group must work away from home to bring in income, someone must care for younger brothers and sisters and help with the household chores. Because they live in areas where trouble may erupt on the streets, inner-city children learn survival tactics and acquire the ability to hide their true feelings. By necessity they become skilled in problem solving.

These are some of the strengths inner-city children contribute to a group. They also contribute "street language" which is functional in their environment for communicating feelings and ideas. If the teacher is from a different environment, it would be advisable for the teacher to become familiar with the "street language" of his or her pupils. The learning materials are probably in "standard" English or use biblical images and may need to be interpreted.

Allow the children to talk out ideas until they have found a way of translating the ideas into terms which make sense to them. In one classroom, the covenant between God and Moses became a "deal."

Inner-city public schools are often crowded, and the children there experience few one-to-one relationships with adults. So, in the church, small group work and a teacher's attention will help to meet this need.

It would not be unusual to find children from well-to-do homes in both the city and suburbs also suffering from lack of attention to their emotional needs, though they are well nourished and well clothed. Their parents tend to have many responsibilities and outside interests.

Children from Puerto Rican, Black, Pennsylvania German, Italian, Native American, and all other cultures have their own family customs, music, and celebrations which they can share with a group. One church school teacher found a wealth of untapped resources when the children were asked to suggest a special way of observing Christmas. It became an international celebration that year; there were food, games, and songs planned by children of varying ethnic backgrounds, with the full cooperation of their families. The teacher reported still another gain from the experience: the children developed increasing esteem in themselves and in their families.

In families where father and mother share equally in the care of children, household duties, and earning a living, children will reflect this influence in their attitudes toward sex roles. Teachers will find cooperation when they can provide learning activities in which boys and girls can choose the activities they want to do, regardless of sex.

Still another environmental influence is exerted by the composition of the family unit. A home does not automatically become a "good" one because it has a mother and a father in residence. There are all kinds of family arrangements: one-parent homes, foster homes, institutions or group homes, adoptive parents, homes where children are living with grandparents, or homes where one or more grandparents reside with the children and their parents. One of the most loving homes we know is composed of a mother, three children, and two grandparents. The grandparents help with the parenting and provide added stability.

Some children may be sensitive when the topic of families arises in a unit of study or an informal discussion. Plan learning activities, including pictures of various home situations and visits by foster parents and other parent figures, to reinforce the idea that all families are acceptable.

Television has helped more than anything to unify our culture. Children in all areas are exposed to the same things via the television set. Viewers learn a great deal, some of it bad and some good. A church school educator has suggested that a dependence on television has resulted in a decreasing ability both to be creative and to use words. "They just prefer to sit," said the teacher. Certainly the impact of television has definite implications for Christian education.

Know Your Children

It is important that you know the environment from which your children come in order to understand and meet their needs. Visit in their homes when possible, both to learn more about the boys and girls and to help parents realize that church school is an important part of the child's life.

While some teachers prefer "drop-in" visits to homes, most parents are in favor of a telephone call to set up the time.

WHAT IF some parents are not interested enough to visit with you and help you learn to know their child?

• You can talk with grandparents or other close relatives if they live nearby. But keep trying to communicate with the parents through occasional personal notes, telephone calls regarding the child's progress, and invitations to special church school events.

Visit public school teachers in order to determine the school's expectations for children of the age you are teaching. Visit a classroom and see the children in action. School plays, art exhibits, and other special events are means of knowing your children better.

Keep a notebook with records about each child in areas such as church school attendance, interests, relationships with other children, what the child does well, accounts of events involving the child, and special needs. Don't trust these things to your memory; reviewing written progress notes will help you to keep abreast of growth and changes taking place in individual children.

The Child Grows in the Christian Faith

Love, understanding, and trust between teachers and pupils is the most effective element of teaching. The Christian faith is communicated, not primarily through facts and verbalization, but through love, concern, forgiveness, and acceptance. A child's sense of worth can be destroyed by mistrust and misunderstanding. A session could deal at length with God's love; but if the teacher exhibits a lack of understanding or hesitancy in accepting a child, what the child learns is not what the session was intended to teach.

Early elementary children think in concrete terms; it is difficult for them to know God, whom they cannot see or touch. But they can relate a loving and caring God to a teacher who shows them these qualities.

They are very literal minded and are unable to make the transition from the real to the symbolic. Pictures and songs of Jesus as a shepherd tell them just that, not that Jesus cared for people *as* a shepherd would care for sheep.

Lack of ability to understand other times and places leads to such choice bits of misinformation as "Pontius, the pilot," pictured in his airplane; God, whose name is Harold ("Hallowed be thy name"); and God who "gave his only *forgotten* son."

The church family is important in the children's religious growth, too. If a child is rejected through a thoughtless remark or action by an adult church member, he or she will be slow to trust again. To the child, these are God's people and God must be like them.

The children's classroom also speaks to them of the concern of the congregation. If it is well equipped and attractive, children will feel they are important to the church.

Here are some religious concepts, in children's language, which are appropriate for the early elementary age child:

• God made everything in our world. • We are part of God's world. • God loves us all the time. • Jesus showed us what God is like. • When we do wrong, God is sad. • When we do wrong, it hurts us and others. • We can count on God. • God forgives us. • All people in the world are part of God's family. • The church is people. • People of God love and help each other. • It is not easy to be the persons God wants us to be. • God helps us. • God always keeps God's promises. • We can love and help others. • God loves me even when I do wrong. • I can forgive others. • People of God worship together. • God plans for a good world. • God is always with us.

2

What Can We Do?

Teaching early elementary children involves far more than putting factual knowledge into fertile young brains. It is:
• Listening to what children tell you with their words, with their eyes, with their actions, with their silence. • Giving assurance to children who are doubtful of their self-worth. • Helping children to discover appropriate behavior. • Answering a question for the tenth time with a smile in your voice. • Remembering and keeping your promises. • Accepting a child's interpretation when you could say it so much better yourself. • Sharing the excitement of a beautiful butterfly—or even a garter snake. • Showing respect for a child's idea. • Communicating without talking down. • Loving even the seemingly unlovable. • Encouraging the children to discover for themselves when it would be much quicker to tell them yourself. • Being patient when everything seems to be going wrong. • Admitting that you don't know the answer either. • Teaching a child to *want* to think, rather than what to think. • Fostering creativity as a response to Creator God. • Not expecting more than a child is capable of doing.

Children will come to know God more readily through a teacher who listens, loves, and explores with them than through a teacher who knows every answer and imparts that knowledge with little love and understanding.

In view of our discussion of the characteristics and abilities of the early elementary child, here are some things to be considered:

Since it is children's God-given nature to be on the move, we need to think of learning as *activity* for the whole child, rather than merely listening and answering questions. Provide numerous opportunities to respond to ideas through art, music, and body movement. This is especially important if some of your children are self-conscious about expressing themselves in words. Thus, you will not feel the need to insist that each individual talk in a discussion or contribute to sentence prayers. When a child has gained sufficient self-esteem or feels comfortable with the class, she or he will contribute verbally without being singled out.

Even though some children will be able to read material which is written for their age level, remember that this is not a reading class! It is not necessary that children practice their reading skills in church school. Going around the circle with each child reading a sentence or a paragraph discourages understanding and encourages anxiety.

If you have children from ethnic backgrounds which are different from those of the majority in the group, work these differences into your session plans in ways which will promote acceptance and appreciation. For instance, you could have a family covered-dish meal, with parents bringing certain foods which are part of their cultural background. If some of the boys and girls come from homes where another language is spoken, they could teach the class some Bible words and phrases from that language.

If you discover children who have given up trying, make an effort to find something which will spark their interest and bring them a measure of success.

Grouping

You may have a class in which all children are in one grade, or your class may include more than one grade. Unless you have a very small number of boys and girls, less than eight, you will need to group them for convenience in working together.

> **WHAT IF** you have only two or three children in a class?
> • You can consider it an opportunity to give individual attention to each one. If they have very different abilities, offer choices of simultaneous learning activities.

It is desirable to have a teacher available to work with each group when it needs assistance. If you are teaching alone, you can recruit parents, senior citizens, and other adults in the congregation to assist when necessary. These persons can share their special skills with the children—for example, music, art, carpentry, dramatics, and so on.

Some groups may be long term, and others temporary. About five to eight children is a good number to group together. In learning activities which require writing and reading comprehension, the children can be grouped according to ability, if this seems to be a good working arrangement. Remember that all children of a particular grade level will not be comparable in abilities. Some second graders will be able to read better than some of the third graders. Some children will be able to work more or less independently while teachers need to give more help to others.

It often works well to have children of different ages and abilities together in the same group. Younger and older children can learn from one another, while the older and more experienced provide their skills so that the work of the group goes more smoothly.

Scheduling

As you plan for each session, list learning activities in the order you expect them to take place, along with the approximate number of minutes each one will probably take. As you do this, however, keep in mind that you are planning for and with *children* and not writing a prescription which must be followed exactly.

Your schedule needs to be flexible. There is no point in continuing a discussion of one thing when the children's minds have wandered to another. The boys and girls will give you cues when they have begun to reach the saturation point. There may be extra wiggling and shuffling of feet, a giggle as one child playfully pokes another, or a question entirely unrelated to the present topic. Don't wait until they have completely lost interest to shift gears; it would be better to stop early and promise that they can resume the activity at another time if anyone wishes. Then suggest a song the children particularly enjoy singing or some other activity planned for later in the session.

When the children first arrive, they probably will be alert and eager. If the children straggle into the teaching area, it provides you with the opportunity to greet them individually. At this time, your schedule should allow for several minutes of individual activity. An early activity on your schedule might be one which requires absorbed attention, such as listening to a story or reviewing ideas from the previous session. This would be followed by something which involves physical activity: informal dramatics, a game, or a song.

Try to alternate quiet and active experiences during the session period. One effective way to signal a change of activity is to turn off the lights for just a moment. Soon the boys and girls will become used to the idea that this means it is time for something different.

By the end of the session, the children may be tired and ready to go home. Make your closing activity one which they can take at their own pace: reflect, internalize, review future plans, evaluate.

Always have more ideas than you need for a session, so that you can substitute another learning activity for one which seems to fall flat. Be alert for ideas proposed by the children, too. Don't ever let them get the idea that you feel it is *your* class! It isn't.

Worship Opportunities

True worship is a sense of feeling close to God and being aware of God's presence. Effective worship grows out of the learning activities of the session. It might happen in response to a story, to an experience in working together, to a discovery the children have made. Thus, it is hardly ever the first item on your schedule.

Occasionally a somewhat formal worship service can be planned by the girls and boys, perhaps at the conclusion of a unit. It could include Bible verses, songs, a litany or a unison prayer which were a part of the study.

Avoid making worship routine, using the same formula from week to week. Never teach a song during the time set aside for worship. Practice for worship is not the same as worship.

Worship doesn't happen always at prescribed times or to each child at once. For young children it sometimes seems to happen spontaneously. Teachers may not even be aware that it is taking place.

Once a group of third graders was walking in the out-of-doors. One of them noticed a bird fluttering around a certain tree, guarding a nest. The children spoke in whispers and kept very quiet so the bird would not be disturbed any further. Soon not a word was spoken. Teacher and children joined in silent praise. It was the children's own discovery and the teacher didn't feel it was necessary to build on the experience with her own interpretation; she just let it happen.

Whether or not an early elementary child can gain from participation in church worship depends upon the child, the congregation, and the church service. Having children sit in a service they don't understand probably won't help them to feel a part of the church. On the other hand, if the adults are loving and welcoming, and some part of the service is meant for children, they would benefit from attending. Church school teachers can prepare the way by talking over the various parts of the service with the children and familiarizing them with hymns, prayers, and responses.

Planning with Children

Even at the early elementary age, children are able to participate in planning their learning activities. The boys and girls help to set goals by indicating their interests and expectations and then suggesting ways of making discoveries.

For example, let's take the unit theme "God Begins God's Family." After the children have looked at pictures which you have displayed and have commented on them, enthusiastically tell them the theme of the unit and ask how the group could find out about God's family. Accept all the ideas and write them on the chalkboard or newsprint. Don't stop to decide whether or not a suggestion is workable; keep those ideas coming.

Now consider these criteria with the children to determine which suggestions will be used: *Will we have time to do this activity? How will it help us make discoveries about God's family? Do we have the equipment or can we get it?* If a suggested idea can't be done, perhaps it can be adapted so that it is more practical.

From the list remaining after you have eliminated the impractical ideas, choose those learning activities which the class thinks would be most interesting and helpful. Next you might ask the children to form small groups to make some plans for each of the selected activities.

Children also should be involved in setting rules and guidelines. They also will be more ready to follow rules they have helped to make and will see that others follow them, too.

A session or a unit is never complete until it has been evaluated for the contribution it has made to the learning group. Children participate in this as they recall discoveries, discuss problems and how they were handled, and make suggestions on how an activity could have accomplished more.

Our Ministry with Parents and Other Adults

Ideally, religious teaching begins in the home and continues in church school. Consider parents as members of a team in the Christian education of their children. We cannot program the home, but we can let parents know that we assume that they want the best for their children. We can ask for their suggestions and offer our ideas of activities to be done at home which will contribute to a child's growth in the faith. While we may not always agree with what is happening in the home, we should never "put down" or belittle a parent to the child.

Take advantage of every opportunity to interpret the early elementary program to adults in the church family. There will be those who observe that the children are moving to music and playing games during sessions and will wonder, perhaps aloud, why the boys and girls are not being taught the plan of salvation or memorizing the Ten Commandments. Listen to these adults with respect and try to keep the lines of communication open. Perhaps they do not realize that you *are* helping children respond to Christ in ways appropriate for them.

Communicate to parents your own beliefs on how learning takes place: that children of this age learn primarily through *relationships* with adults who love and serve God. At first, children believe because they see the Christian faith at work through the lives of other people. They are not mature enough as yet to comprehend abstract concepts. So we provide here-and-now, see-and-touch experiences for children to enable them to test out ideas and repeatedly practice Christian principles. It is useless (or worse) to try to teach children something they will need in the future if it is not meaningful at the moment. Early elementary children have a great desire to please adults. We must not exploit their needs to please adults by encouraging them to make decisions for Christ before they are able to understand much of what such a decision involves.

Why not invite adults who question what is happening in your class to visit regularly and, perhaps in keeping with your session plans, share their interests and skills with the children?

3

How Can We Do It?

In light of the needs, interests, and abilities of children of early elementary age, here are some learning activities which will be effective in sharing the Christian faith.

Taking Trips

The trips your children take can be within the church building to visit the sanctuary, the library, the church office; to talk with the organist; to discover the date on the cornerstone; or to admire and study the stained-glass windows.

Trips may be taken into the community: to visit shut-ins, a synagogue, or another church; to go to the hospital, police station, or fire company to see how others care for our needs; to visit a children's home or geriatric center to bring cheer to other people.

Wherever you go inside the church or in the community, make your plans in advance and ask the person in authority whether or not you may come and when would be a convenient time for the visit. There must be a purpose for each trip, and the person who is being visited should be informed of that purpose, the age level of the children, how many might be expected, and what they will want to discover.

The children also must be prepared for the trip. Tell them what they can expect to see and hear and help them to think of questions they may want to ask. Discuss the importance of rules and let them be the ones to suggest the rules which will be in effect during the trip. These should cover staying together, crossing streets, and being courteous to those persons whom they meet.

You may need to recruit parents or other adults in the church if you are taking a trip outside the church building. And do obtain the permission of the parents of each child for such excursions.

One of the teachers should be prepared to take notes on what is learned to help the children to recall information and observations later. The trip is not over until the children have had the opportunity to review their discoveries and evaluate their experiences. The trips might culminate with stories composed by the boys and girls, accounts prepared for the church newsletter, letters of appreciation to those persons who were visited, and perhaps service projects inspired by needs they may have discovered.

Service Projects

With their naturally sympathetic and friendly natures, children will want to do things to help others. They can be helped to see that Christians help others in response to God's love. Of course, there are national and international projects in which they can take part, but it seems better for them to do things in their own community where they can participate in person. To do so is in keeping with their need for concrete experiences, and it makes the activity much more satisfying to the girls and boys.

Sharing projects do not always have to involve material gifts. The sharing of time and talents with a lonely person is even more important than material objects.

A service project might begin with a trip to let the children see for themselves what is needed. A visit to a children's home or day-care center might result in a party prepared by both groups; some lasting friendships may begin.

Whatever the service project, attitudes toward those outside the group will be involved. Teachers need to be aware of their own attitudes and motivations; they are readily caught by children. Some ways to foster positive attitudes are: • Thinking of persons as individuals (somebody's grandma, some mother's child), rather than as large groups. • Desiring to make new friends. • Being open to differences, rather than expecting people to be "just like us." • Being mindful of the worth of persons, their contributions to society. • Having love, rather than pride or self-satisfaction, as the reason for doing service.

Storytelling

Preparing to read or tell a story to children requires practice so that storytellers are confident enough to put themselves into the tale, conveying excitement and enjoyment to the listeners.

Some teachers feel it is necessary to study the story over and over so that it can be told to the children without using the book. Other teachers feel more confident with the book in front of them, perhaps adding details to create more interest. If you use this method, become thoroughly familiar with the story so that you can maintain eye contact with the children during a large share of the time. If attention wavers, ask a question to rekindle interest or adjust the pace of the story. Experience will teach you how long a story will hold your listeners' attention.

Don't give away the whole point of the story in introducing it. When it is finished, add no explanations or morals; a well-told story explains itself and gives a child something to think about in days to come. Ask questions to provoke thought, such as: *How do you feel about what the boy did?* or *What would you have done if this happened to you?*

Sometimes you will want to make up your own stories or adapt other stories so they relate better to the children's own situations.

Conversation and Discussion

Stories are often followed by discussion. When you ask children how they feel about something or what they would do, be prepared to accept the answers without negative comments or raised eyebrows. One of your primary responsibilities in conversing with children is to create a climate in which they feel free to express their own ideas and opinions without the fear of being ridiculed. You can do this by taking them seriously when they ask a question or express feelings and by accepting their ideas as worthy of consideration.

Sometimes you will ask a question and will be greeted by complete silence. Perhaps there was an unfamiliar word or expression in your question. If you think this might be the case, try again, substituting a simpler word or giving a brief explanation. If you still don't get a response, let it go with, "Perhaps we'll talk about that later."

Sometimes children answer your questions with what they think you want to hear instead of their own opinions. If you suspect this is happening, review your own question and your attitude as you asked it. Do you think your attitude conveyed the idea that you wanted a certain answer? How can you enable children to express their thoughts freely? For now, accept the child's answer as it was given you.

The surest way of stopping a conversation is to ask a question which can be answered with a simple "Yes" or "No." If these questions can't be avoided, follow them immediately with, "Why do you think so?"

Music

Music in the church school class is more than just learning the words and tune of a song and then singing it. It can include a visit with the organist who shows the children how the organ works and sounds, a visit from various instrumentalists, listening to recordings of hymns of the church or theme music, perhaps painting to the sound of recorded music, creating a song, or using rhythm instruments. Music evokes feelings: happiness, sadness, thoughtfulness. It is a way of communicating without words.

Children enjoy singing melodies which are lively, simple, and familiar. Try having your boys and girls create their own songs by putting words to nursery rhymes or television commercials. This could be done in response to a story. Bible verses can be sung to familiar tunes, too.

It is recommended that you use a song chart in teaching a song, even if the words are printed in the children's books. A chart helps to focus the eyes of the girls and boys on the teacher who is directing the tempo and on her other hand which shows them the words. The words should be printed in manuscript style, capital and small letters, with which the children have become familiar in public school.

WHAT IF you do not sing or play an instrument?
- You can invite someone to class who can teach the song, or you can prerecord it on tape so you can use it later as a teaching device.

Informal Dramatization

Acting the part of another person gives children a better understanding of how that person feels and helps them to become aware of the person's problems and needs.

The children can use informal dramatization both as a way to recall a story and as a way to express their different solutions to an open-ended story. Puppet play is useful in expressing feelings, for this allows the children to detach themselves from the situation, thinking and talking as the puppets, with less self-consciousness.

Informal dramatization with early elementary children differs greatly from putting on a play. There are several advantages and few of the problems. No stage is needed. There is probably little in the way of scenery and costumes, but there are a lot of imaginary props and unrehearsed dialogue.

Unrehearsed does not mean that there is not preparation. After the children and teacher have read and discussed the story which will be acted out, the boys and girls decide which character each will play. They talk over how this character would act and how she or he might talk. There is no written dialogue. The children make it up as they go along, based on their understanding of the characters and the events.

Ask questions like these: *What kind of a person is this character? What do you think she would do? How would she act toward the other persons? How would she talk?*

Try tape-recording the play so the children can listen to it and comment on the activity later in the session.

Creative Art

Creative art activities, using a variety of media, allow children to express themselves freely. Through creative art they can express their feelings, their ideas—what the world looks like to them. When they illustrate a Bible story, they may be able to let you know what about it impressed them. Children, with their gradually developing small muscles and hand-eye coordination, may not produce a final work which is perfect in your eyes or theirs. This should not trouble you because you will not be looking for perfection but for the joy of individual expression.

Before you introduce a new creative art idea to your class, try it out yourself. Leave the sample at home or in the cupboard though, or children may take the path of least resistance and try to copy the sample. What we really want is for each child to respond in his or her own individual way.

WHAT IF there's no time for creative art?
• You need to rethink how the class spends its time. What are the children doing?

Puppets may be created for the children to use in dramatic play; table scenes or dioramas may be created to visualize scenes in stories or people and places in a study; collages and finger painting may be used to express feelings; friezes and murals can tell stories; any variety of pictures can be made to visualize ideas or help recall what has been studied.

Conclude the activity by giving the boys and girls an opportunity to display their work and tell what it means to them.

Creative Writing

Creative writing is a way in which children can put together their ideas and discover meanings. Younger children will probably work better in a group with a teacher serving as a recorder as they dictate their ideas. Boys and girls with greater abilities in writing and expressing themselves might work individually.

Activities may include writing letters, invitations, stories, poetry, prayers, litanies, and reports of trips or visits.

Perhaps the easiest to begin with would be a letter to someone who has helped in a unit of study. Suggest that the children recall some of the interesting things they saw and heard and mention these in the letter.

Jot down these ideas on the chalkboard or a large sheet of paper as the children express them. Don't try to improve on the ideas; let this be an expression of their own thoughts. It will be more satisfying to the boys and girls and more appreciated by the recipient. Then ask the girls and boys to decide how the ideas will be put together in the letter in its finished form.

The use of a tape recorder might be even more stimulating to the children's imaginations, since they would not have to worry about the mechanics of spelling and putting words on paper.

Outdoor Opportunities

There are many learning opportunities available in the out-of-doors which just can't be duplicated in a classroom. When the weather is suitable, you could move the class outside for a complete session. At other times you could have picnics, walks, and perhaps an afternoon at a farm.

WHAT IF your church is in the city?

• You can use backyards, city parks, and sidewalk cracks to observe signs of life, such as ants and blades of grass. Use rooftops to observe the clouds, wind blowing, and shadows in the sunshine.

Leave schedules behind in the classroom, for they won't work on an exploring trip. You can't plan to look at a butterfly at 9 A.M. and then find a bird's nest at 9:30 A.M. And you don't go on talking about ants and ignore the bird which has just lighted on a nearby branch and is entertaining the children with a lovely melody.

Learning Center Approach

This approach, featuring a variety of resources made available at designated centers, offers opportunities for children to learn at their own individual pace, according to their individual interests.

During most of the session time the children will be moving through the learning centers of their choice, completing one activity and moving to another. At times they will come together to share the results of their activities.

Centers can be set up as skill areas: music, drama, art, audio-visuals, books, conversation, cooking, games, nature. They can also be set up for exploring topics related to the unit of study. Those centers which contribute to the achievement of the group's goals and those which provide opportunities for the children to pursue their interests are the most important.

In some centers there will be resources for discovering facts; in others there will be resources for exploring feelings and for responding creatively to new ideas.

The teacher's role in the learning center approach is to serve as a resource or enabler. This approach is made to order for a teacher who is working alone with the group. The children do not learn just from the teacher; they learn from resources in the centers and from each other. The teacher circulates among the learning centers, making sure things are going well, stopping for conversation with one group of children, helping another find information.

Job cards can be placed at the centers, giving instructions to the girls and boys. For nonreaders, instructions could be ready on a cassette tape. Instructions for the dramatic center might be: • Listen to the first story on the tape. • How do you think it should end? • Make up an end for the story. • Act it out. • Talk about the ending. • Go on to the next story.

If you have a small room, learning centers can be set up in corners, under tables, almost anywhere where there is space for three or four children and the resources needed for them to accomplish their learning tasks. More ideas for creating learning centers in small classrooms can be found in the book, *Nooks, Crannies and Corners*, listed in the resource list on pages 62 and 63.

Groups at Work

There is no established way of organizing groups; but once children are assigned to a group, it is the task of a teacher and each one of the children to build it into an effective community. A climate of mutual confidence must be established so that each member feels free to be himself or herself and knows that he or she will be accepted. In this kind of group, ideas can be expressed without fear of ridicule; suggestions for change can be accepted; caring can be expressed. The most valuable asset of a group is the variety of talents which exists within it. Individual members teach each other and help each other; often it is the adult teacher who learns most of all through interaction with the children.

Teachers can foster a cohesive group by giving the boys and girls freedom to make decisions and settle problems to the best of their abilities. The teacher acts as another member of the group. Conflicts are brought out in the open where they can be dealt with and eliminated. This is how children learn to live with each other and develop mutual respect.

4

What Do We Need?

Space and Equipment

Teachers don't often have control over the amount of space in their classrooms. This is determined by the construction of the building and the assignment of rooms. We'll talk here about some general standards of space and suggest ways of expanding it by occasional use of other facilities.

The younger the child, the more space is required for physical activity. We've already pointed out how much early elementary children need to move around; learning is inhibited by too much sitting still. The usual standard for the early elementary age is thirty-five square feet per child. This does not include such areas as bathrooms and storage facilities.

Before you throw up your hands in despair, saying you don't have sufficient space to begin to teach, let's consider some ways to add to your facilities. You might arrange from time to time to use the fellowship hall or a hallway for games, the kitchen for cooking and creative art, and the library, church parlor, choir room, or pastor's study for reading and browsing. You can use the outdoors as additional space. Perhaps a private home would be available during your church school class time. In addition, you might schedule extra sessions during the week when the church building is less crowded. Learning can take place in a small room or the back pew of the sanctuary, as well as in an ideal classroom.

If possible, the class should be held in an area of the building separated from adult groups who might be disturbed by singing and other noise-producing activities. It isn't fair to restrict children too much as they work and play. Usually the classroom which buzzes with voices and activity is the one where the most effective learning is taking place.

The teaching area should be attractively arranged so that it says to children, "Come in. You are welcome here. We care about you." The location of furniture and equipment must allow freedom of movement.

There should be child-sized tables and chairs, arranged in face-to-face groupings as opposed to rows. Chairs which fold increase the probability of squeezed fingers and falls. Part of the floor, covered by a fairly thick and washable rug, can serve as a storytelling and conversation area. Try to have a worship table with an open Bible and perhaps flowers of the season and pictures.

Ideally you should have open shelves where supplies are readily accessible to the learners: pencils, paper, paste, crayons, blunt-edged scissors, and so on. It would be a good idea to provide individual space for each child's working materials, including his or her learner's book. This could be a large manila envelope or perhaps a plastic tray with the child's name printed on it. You will also need paint jackets, smocks, or used men's shirts to protect clothing.

Other desirable equipment might include:

• A chalkboard or a place where large sheets of paper (such as unprinted newspaper or butcher paper) can be hung for jotting down ideas expressed by the children.

• A bulletin board which should be kept attractive and timely. Place it at the child's eye level.

• A chest where dress-up clothes can be stored.

Printed Resources

Have several Bibles, but not necessarily as many as one for each learner. A modern-language translation is easier for children to understand, but be cautious in using paraphrases of the Bible. Some paraphrases are slanted toward the writer's personal interpretations.

In choosing other suitable books for children, consider these factors: • They should be at the reading levels of the children and should be attractively illustrated. • Biblical illustrations should be authentic. • Books should not define certain sex roles, such as illustrating only girls caring for dolls or only boys playing the role of police officer. • Some books can be just for fun; others should be the kind which help children to understand their own life situations and solve problems. You also will want to have books which help the children learn about the life and teachings of Jesus and how God works in our world.

You could borrow books from the children's section of the public library. Perhaps the boys and girls would like to bring some of their own books to class to share with others.

Audiovisual Resources

Save all the teaching pictures which are part of the teaching-learning resources used by your class and keep them in a picture file for future use. The file can be as simple as a large cardboard carton. If the pictures are not on cardboard, mount them so they will remain in good condition.

There will be occasions when you will need present-day pictures and you may not be able to locate suitable ones on short notice. As you look through magazines, keep an eye out for pictures which illustrate concepts suitable for use with your children. Clip and mount them to add to your picture file.

Number each picture on the reverse side and keep the pictures in order. Set up a card-index file by subject matter to make it easier to locate the pictures when you need them. Cards might contain this type of information:

CHRISTMAS—Biblical No. _____

    Nativity Scene—black and white.

    Size _____

CHRISTMAS—Modern   No. _____

Children's choir in front of Christmas tree. Color.

Size _____

A record player which children can operate, selected recordings, rhythm instruments, and perhaps an autoharp are suitable.

You probably will want to use a filmstrip projector on occasion, but this might be considered general church school equipment which would be shared by all the classes. Unless your church school has a library of filmstrips, you will need to order these from your denominational headquarters. Be sure to allow three to four weeks for delivery of filmstrips. This means advance planning!

A Polaroid camera and tape recorder are other pieces of equipment which would be useful in some units of study. These can be brought from home when they are needed.

People in the Community as Resources

The following are some resources which may be located in your community which could be of help in providing or contributing to learning activities. Public library and school librarians could help to evaluate reading materials for the children. A geriatric center, day-care center, and similar institutions would welcome visits from the girls and boys. Other churches and a synagogue would provide learning opportunities for discovering how other people in the community worship. The police and fire departments as well as the hospital could help the children discover how help is given to people who need it. From your own knowledge of your community, you are sure to find other valuable resources.

People in the Church Family as Resources

All of the people in the church family can serve as resources for your children. Elderly persons can tell the boys and girls what the church was like in former days and share their personal experiences. The organist and choir members can share their musical talents and help the children learn hymns. The minister can share his or her experiences in visiting persons who are sick or shut in and other things which would be interesting to the children. If you are so fortunate as to have a church library, the librarian can show the boys and girls how to find books and other resources. The janitor can tell them what she or he does to keep the church building comfortable and clean. The possibilities are endless. Inviting people in the church family to be a part of your learning activities can help to support the children's feeling of belonging.

You, as a member of the church family, are a key resource in teaching children. In you and others God's Spirit is at work in ministering to and with early elementary children.

5

Our Ministry with Children

Our ministry is guiding children in their Christian growth. It is a ministry that can happen at different times and in many ways. Sometimes it takes place in the church school class, on camping retreats, on visits to shut-ins, during family events, while working together on projects or creative activities, in experiences of discovery, or while sharing in play. The possibilities for ministry are endless. However it happens, our ministry with children focuses on the nurturing of the *child's awareness of and response to God.*

Let's look at some things we can do to help us be more effective in this ministry.

Affirm each child as a person of worth. This is a good place to begin! The message of our ministry is that God loves all people. God is accepting, forgiving, and loving, and God wants us to grow and respond to that love. A child is better able to understand God's love when he or she experiences love and acceptance from others.

Before we can affirm children in honest ways, we need to know each child well. No two children are alike! Think about the boys and girls with whom you work. List the ways each child in your group is different from the others. Some of the differences you might be aware of are:

- how they are growing.
- abilities they have.
- their willingness to try new things.
- what they understand to be good behavior.
- how they get along with persons their own age.
- how they feel about themselves.

How do we affirm a child? Sometimes affirmation is spoken, such as: "That was good thinking, John." "I'm glad you asked that question!" "Keep using your imagination, Beth. It is good to find different ways of doing things." "Good work!" "How well you two work together!" Each child has something we can encourage from time to time.

There are many unspoken ways to affirm children, such as:
- helping two children settle an argument.
- showing tender care in caring for any physical needs.
- helping an older child find information about a question that seems important.
- giving a hug when it is needed (or even when it is not).

- taking time to listen to a child tell about "wild imaginings," that might make little sense to you.

In whatever way we show affirmation, the child needs to feel we are saying, "You are all right! You are important to me!"

It is easy to affirm children who are happy and always seem to do the right thing. But how does one respond to children who are difficult? Jill throws spitballs whenever she can. Bill withdraws from the class and only wants to stare out of the window. Marge is a disturbance in any group activity and distracts other children. Steve is a tease.

Children need to know that they are accepted and loved even

though what they do is rejected. It is best to separate what the child *does* from what the child *is*. We can do this by avoiding "put downs" or "personal threats." Rather than saying, "Jane, you always cause trouble," or "You can't come back if you do that again!" speak to the child in a way that says you trust him or her to correct the action. For example, "Let's see how we can have a better time."

A child who disturbs others or withdraws from the group has a reason for doing so. Think about why the child is acting in a disturbing way. Is it a need for attention? Is it boredom? Does the child need someone else in the group with whom to work or play? Help the child gain attention in positive ways. For example, find a way for an older child to share his or her special abilities in the learning activities. Enlist the help of a younger child in caring for plants in the room. Show your trust in the child's ability to help and cooperate in a situation. See "Resources" in the back of the book for reading material related to discipline problems.

Children will be more open to being aware of God and responding to God when they experience self-worth in the Christian community.

Create an environment which demonstrates warmth, trust, and care. The environment is people, the feelings in a situation, the room, the activities that happen. The environment is all that surrounds and influences a person. Children are influenced most by the persons who care for them. The place where children gather can also give out good feelings.

A well-lighted, comfortable room helps to build positive attitudes toward the Christian community. On entering a room, a child immediately senses whether he or she wants to be there. When there are things to touch and look at, displays of things children have done, and a promise of activities that will take place, a child wants to get involved. On the other hand, a child does not have much interest if the room is immaculate, sterile, and looks as if nothing exciting could ever happen there. In an inviting environment, whether it is in a space filled with church pews or in someone's living room, the good news of God's love can be felt and experienced before and while it is talked about.

Guide toward an understanding of the Christian faith. This has to do with the message we have to share. It centers in the Bible as a record of God's action among persons in the past, God's revelation in Jesus Christ, and God's action through the Holy Spirit and in the Christian community today.

Through the years we want children to gain a knowledge of the events and people of the Bible. As they grow older, so may their understanding of God's message in the Bible deepen and become a resource for their living. Sharing the message also means guiding a child's growth toward a commitment to the sovereignty of Jesus Christ. The child is able at different stages of development to discover meaning in the life and teachings of Jesus that will help in relationships and decision making. Learning about God's activity through the people of God in the past and within the Christian community today is important.

To grow in knowing about and experiencing the Christian faith is a lifelong task. This is expressed in the following statement.

The objective of the church's educational ministry is that all persons be aware of God through God's self-disclosure, especially God's redeeming love as revealed in Jesus Christ, and, enabled by the Holy Spirit, *respond in faith and love;* that as new persons in Christ they may *know* who they are and what their human situation means, *grow* as children of God rooted in the Christian community, *live* in obedience to the will of God in every relationship, *fulfill* their common vocation in the world, and *abide* in the Christian hope [1] (author's italics).

This objective has special importance to our ministry with children. In one sense, it spells out the basic goal of Christian education. Yet, there are no "pat answers"; there is no single way of acting or thinking that must be learned. It does not assume that by a particular age or grade a child will know certain information and facts. Nor does it assume that a person's awareness of God or a particular response to God will happen at any one time in life. The objective has an openness that allows for varying degrees in awareness of God and response to God at each stage of a person's growth.

For the child, the difference will be in terms of individual development, readiness, and experience.

Becky, for example, watches her cat give birth to kittens and then care for them fastidiously. As a result of watching her pet, Becky begins to think about what life is and how animals and humans know how to care for themselves. At this point of her interest, Becky's understanding of God as Creator and Provider may begin to take shape. Becky has an experience which makes her ready to ask questions and understand meaning.

On the other hand, there is Jimmy who is the same age as Becky

---

[1] *Foundations for Curriculum* (Valley Forge: Board of Educational Ministries, American Baptist Churches, U.S.A., 1966), p. 13.

and in her class at school. Jimmy knows the church as the place he is told what he "ought" to do or "ought not to do." He is afraid of being rejected at church. Jimmy's ideas of God are shaped by his experiences there. Jimmy has difficulty becoming aware of a loving God and responding to God with gratitude and love.

The objective of the church's educational ministry has an interesting characteristic. It assumes growth. Each of us from the youngest child to the oldest adult may continue to grow in any of the points mentioned in the objective. The degree of our awareness of God and response to God will differ depending on our maturity and experience. This is the experience of growing and becoming in the Christian faith.

A Shared Ministry

Your teaching task is one part of a larger ministry with children. This nurturing ministry is shared with the entire congregation. Many congregations make a commitment when parents' dedicate their children in an act of worship. At this time a promise is made to support the parents and to provide various ways to help the child to grow in Christian love.

Christian congregations are responding to the needs of children in a variety of practical and creative ways. Churches are providing nursery schools, kindergarten classes, day-care centers for working parents, and programs for children in need of special education. Some after-school programs offer opportunities in creative expression through art, music, and drama. Other churches provide space and leadership for community clubs, libraries, and athletic programs. Many church school classes are moving to an afternoon or evening time when it is more convenient for children and adult workers to gather. Camping, weekend retreats, or backpacking trips for older children have become favorite ways to involve adult leaders, young people, and older children informally in sharing the Christian faith. There are many possibilities in a nurturing ministry.

Not only are events and programs planned specifically for children; but also, whenever possible, children are involved with adults in meaningful ways in the total life of the congregation. Such participation is where children come to know Christianity as a way of life to be lived.

As children share with others in worship, fun times, fellowship events, in the sharing-caring ways people help each other, they will come to experience the church as a community of faith through whom God works today.

What You Can Do

Have you ever wondered, "Why am I here? What is the purpose? What will I teach? How will I do it?" In our ministry with children it is not only *what* we teach, but also *the child* whom we teach that is important.

As a teacher your role will be that of a guide and a resource person. You are not expected to be an expert who has all the information to give to children. You will invite the children to learn by providing an opportunity, stimulating their interest, providing resources and guidance, sharing your faith. You will learn along with them and from them! You will help children to think about what they have learned and what meaning it has for their lives.

Look again at the statement of objective on page 37. You will notice that it not only gives direction to our ministry with children, but also we may use it as a check on what we are doing. It can help us evaluate what is happening with children. We can ask ourselves: *What difference does this session or activity make to the child in moving along the lifetime objective of being aware of God? How does it help the child grow toward responding to God?*

You Are Not Alone

Considering our ministry with children may leave you with the feeling "How can I do it all?" There are others who share this responsibility.

Usually an elected group cares for the total program of Christian education within a local church. Their responsibility is to provide leadership, space for activities, and resource materials as well as to make decisions about children's activities. They will count on you to let them know when you have needs in any of these areas. Perhaps you would like to have training in teaching skills. Or you may think there is a need for a particular activity, such as a children's choir. This committee will make the decision on these activities and help to facilitate them.

The pastor also shares this responsibility for ministry with children. There are many ways a pastor can help: talking over your teaching situation with you, coming to observe what you are doing, helping you in teaching an idea, being one of the teaching team for a couple of sessions, directing you to resources to help in your teaching. This person may welcome an opportunity to work with you.

Other persons in the church share your task. Those responsible for "outreach" or contacting unchurched people may visit families of children who do not belong to the church. Committees working with mission activities can include the children in planning and carrying out specific mission projects. Adult church school classes may provide transportation, counselors for camping experiences, or they may share in service projects. Parents may form a study group to discuss the themes you are working with in order to find ways to reinforce learnings in the family. Parents might also take turns as "teaching aides" when needed.

The planned and spontaneous ways of ministering with children ultimately depend on the work of the Holy Spirit. The objective of Christian education describes the work of the Holy Spirit as an "enabling force." As the spirit of the child is moved by the Holy Spirit, he or she may respond in faith and enter into fellowship with God in Christ.

The Holy Spirit will enable you as a teacher to have the power, strength, and love to provide an open, inviting teaching-learning situation in your ministry with children.

6

Children and Learning

How Children Learn in the Church

Children learn in the church essentially the same way they learn in any other place. Let us look at five important considerations in the process of learning.

Children are able to learn when they are ready—physically, emotionally, socially, intellectually. We do not expect a nursery child to do the same kind of playing or thinking that we expect of a kindergarten child or a first grader. We need to be aware of the characteristics of growth stages, so that we can help children learn at their own point of readiness.

For example, think about Mary, a nursery child. When she is expected to hold a Bible and repeat a memory verse in church school, she may learn that the book is heavy, has small black things, and strange pictures on the page. Mary may also learn that the book is very important to the teacher. The verse she repeats makes the teacher happy. Mary has not yet developed in her ability to understand the meaning of the verse. Mary's language development is limited. She can repeat what someone else tells her to, but that does not mean that she understands the meaning. Mary thinks in intuitive and pre-logical rather than abstract ways. She may be able to say through imitation, "Jesus loves me," or "God loves me." She better understands "Mommy loves baby " as she sees her mother care for the baby. Plan for all children, nursery age as well as older children, to learn in ways that fit their abilities.

Each child is different. Some have abilities and experiences that others do not have. Susan and Cliff are in the fifth grade. Susan has moved with her family many times and makes friends easily. Susan has little difficulty taking part in a group discussion about *how* Jesus' teachings can apply to relationships in her school life. Cliff is quiet, tends to be withdrawn from the group, and is artistic. Cliff is uncomfortable discussing Jesus' teachings with others. On the other hand, he is able to think through meaning as he illustrates a comic strip. Individual differences make it important for us to understand each child in terms of that child's own unique characteristics and readiness to learn.

Children want to learn when they have a need to learn or an experience that stimulates them to learn.

Take Cory as an example. Cory tries again and again to ride his brother's two-wheel bike, but his legs are not long enough to reach the pedals. He does not yet have the coordination or balance to ride the bicycle. When Cory is physically able to learn this skill, he will do so quickly. Then he will have the ability to match his desire to learn.

A child may be mature enough to learn a particular skill, but unless he or she sees a reason for it, there will not be as much interest to learn. A group of sixth graders visited a shut-in as a part of a study on the mission of the church. They talked with her about what they did in school, their pets and hobbies, and some of their activities in church school. In turn, she shared with them memories of early days when the town was only a village and the church consisted of two families meeting in a home. It was an exciting visit for both the children and

the shut-in. Afterwards, as they talked about the visit, an idea grew for a project to care for shut-ins in their church and neighborhood. **Children learn best when they are involved** in the learning process. Learning is not like a spectator sport. The learner has to take part in it to make it happen. It is not enough to sit by and watch a well-prepared teacher do his or her own thing. Let's look at some ways to involve children in their learning.

Usually, you set goals to clarify your own purpose for teaching. Share these goals with the children. They want to know what they are going to do and why. "In this session (or in the next few weeks), we are going to be thinking about. . . ."

Better still, involve the children in setting the goals. The extent to which children can share in planning depends on their age and ability to do so. We can involve children by finding out what they already know and what their questions are. It may take some time to talk with the children and listen to their ideas. When learners make plans for themselves and the group, care needs to be taken to be sure they are realistic. Think through together such questions as: *Where can we find out information? Whom do we know who could help us? How much time do we have to do this? What activities could we do to help us understand and express the meaning?*

Learners become interested when they are a part of the decision making and carrying out of the plans. Children may also be involved through exploring, finding answers to their questions, working out an idea through activities, and evaluating. The sixth graders described earlier became involved in many ways. They made a visit in which they shared their own interests and activities; they evaluated the visit and then planned and carried out a project.

Involving the children in what happens encourages them to develop self-confidence and to understand their own abilities.

Children learn best when they can relate what they are learning to their own lives.

The team of teachers in one kindergarten class felt satisfied with the completion of a unit around the theme "Friendship." They had used several activities, including dictating stories and illustrating them, dramatizing Bible stories with puppets, sharing with senior citizen friends in the church. They were especially glad to observe Ellen, who was shy and withdrawn, beginning to accept another child as a friend. One day some of the children were building in a learning center. Ellen accidently knocked down the building project. The children were angry and there was some cruel name calling. Ellen seemed to shrink away. The teachers looked at each other in despair. Their looks said,

"What have we been teaching all these weeks?" In a careful way they talked over with the children what had happened. Allowing feelings to be expressed, the teachers showed they understood how disappointed the children felt. They also helped them understand how Ellen felt and how the name calling hurt her.

After the session, the teachers evaluated what had happened. These are some of their findings:

1. They had assumed the children were friends and did not need to grow in relating to each other. The emphasis in the activities had been on friendship with others outside the group.

2. Learning is more than covering the material in a book.

3. Learning takes a long time and a lot of patience. Repetition of an idea is necessary for it to become a part of a person's life.

4. Learning happens when children apply what they talk about and do to their own real-life situations.

Children learn in a variety of ways. Children do have different learning abilities. They learn at different rates of speed and in different ways.

Amy, a fourth grader, is first to say, "What do I do now?" She finishes her art work first. Tom has not developed the ability to cut well. He will be last to finish his work on the project. Amy cannot read well, but Tom reads several grade levels ahead of his own grade. A variety of approaches to teaching will allow Amy and Tom to learn in their own personal ways and give each child a successful feeling about learning.

A few of the many approaches to help children learn are through seeing—pictures, maps, films, chalkboards; hearing—stories, music, records, people sharing experiences, singing, reading; doing—research activities, creative activities (art, drama, role play), discussing, taking field trips, carrying out service activities.

Learning is a personal thing. Each person takes from a situation that which she or he needs or wants and is able to take. In planning for our ministry with children, we need to know each child well. Then we plan opportunities in which that child has the freedom to learn about God's love and respond to that love.

How Children Grow in the Christian Faith

Growing in the Christian faith is a gradual process that continues through life. It is personal. It is based on a child's unique growth patterns and experiences. As we try to understand how the child grows physically, socially, emotionally, and intellectually, we need to apply the same understanding to the child's religious growth. One

way to categorize development in the Christian faith is in terms of
 . . . feeling
  . . . thinking
   . . . acting out.
Growing in the Christian faith cannot be separated from what the child experiences and how the child perceives or understands those experiences.

Feeling

Let us take Mike as an example. Mike comes from outside the Christian community. He is a bright fifth grader who is functioning far below his ability in public school. Mike has had a stormy childhood. He lives with his mother and third stepfather together with other children from three marriages. The father and mother have never had stable employment. They live marginally in a crowded two-room house. Mike's mother is quick to criticize him and punish him physically. Mike has never known security, loving care, or trust. One day he attended a neighborhood church with a friend. He did not understand the sermon, but he did feel the warmth and acceptance of the adults. These feelings led him to return. Mike thinks about God in terms of fear and punishment; these ideas have grown out of his experiences. From what Mike picks up from television and other sources, he associates Jesus and religion with magic.

Mike's Christian growth hinges on his gaining feelings of trust and stability in his world. Before he can move on to thinking about God as love, he needs to be able to count on others. He will need to experience love that is forgiving when he fails. The first step in faith-growth is the feeling of trust, love, and acceptance. This is a need of the youngest baby in the nursery to the oldest child.

The feeling that one is a person of worth is also important. Each child is in the process of testing out who he or she is in the world. The baby asserts herself or himself by announcing a need by crying. Older children test their strength by climbing trees or rebelling against their parents. They are in search of who they are. They need to feel their own identity apart from the family and as a part of their own age group. The church family can help children to grow in self-confidence and self-acceptance. As children are enabled to relate to teachers and other boys and girls, to explore, to use their own initiative and make choices, they have a chance to develop feelings of self-worth. When children are growing in these feelings, they are also growing in their ability to respond to God through Christ.

When a child experiences trust and acceptance in the church

family, he or she may feel that these are people who love. Before children are able to know what the Christian faith is all about, they may feel they are members of a church family. As they share in the worship and informal gatherings, they may feel that these are people who stand for something. These positive feelings about the people of God become associated with the Christian faith. Positive feelings will lead children to grow on the "thinking level" in the Christian faith.

Thinking

"Thinking" about the faith begins early in life when the smallest child asks questions. The questions are prompted by what the child sees, such as a picture of Jesus with the children, or the passing of the offering plate in the worship service, or family members saying grace before meals.

The ability of children to "think" about religion coincides with their intellectual development. At each stage of life, each child has a special way of looking at the world and explaining it in terms of his or her "own set of eyes." The youngest children understand everything in relation to what is happening to them. ("I like chocolate pudding!" "Thank you, God, for chocolate pudding!") Elementary children tend to think in concrete, literal ways. They can understand Jesus who was a child like them or as a man who really lived. Older elementary children are only beginning to think in abstract, symbolic ways about religion. As children grow in ability to think, meanings of the Christian faith will be easier to grasp.

Ideas of the Christian faith are easier to understand when the person "thinks" about them as they are related to life experience. Take the Bible, for example. Some older children are able to memorize Psalm 23. The language of this poem is beautiful and symbolic. When children study Psalm 23 from the point of view of how a Palestinian shepherd lived, they may be able to understand the danger, the feelings of aloneness, thankfulness, and dependence on God that a shepherd might feel. As the children discuss the psalm in relation to the times when they themselves feel danger, aloneness, thankfulness, and a need to depend on others and God, the meaning will be clearer. Only after "thinking" about the meaning of the passage will the truth be learned.

Church school teachers sometimes share too much, too soon with children. They sometimes feel an urgency to tell children more about the Christian faith than they have a capacity to understand. A good test of what you are expecting of children on the "thinking" level is whether you can translate the ideas into the language and experience of the age of the children with whom you are working. Children grow in their ability to understand the faith as they grow intellectually.

Acting Out

Children operate on an "acting" level in Christian growth when they determine their own behavior. This happens when a child moves from imitating others or doing what is expected by others to a point of "acting" because he or she believes it is right to do. A kindergartner may share a puzzle with a new child out of genuine desire to be a friend to the newcomer. That's growth! An older child may resist a temptation to cheat out of conviction rather than a sense of "ought" or "fear." That's acting out Christian values.

Jesus set the example in teaching by asking many questions to make his followers "think" about how they would "act out" biblical meanings in their lives. The decision for "acting out" the Christian faith rests with an individual child. The action will be stimulated by how that child "feels" and "thinks" about his or her own life circumstances and how he or she wants to respond to God.

Children with Special Needs

Children with special needs may have physical, mental, and/or emotional characteristics that differ from those of other children. How can you plan in the church school for Tom, whose hearing is impaired; or Susie, who is blind; or Chris, who is mentally retarded; or Jim, whose emotional problems are the cause for disruption Sunday after Sunday; or Peter, the bright, gifted child? Tom, Susie, Chris, Jim, Peter—each has a right and a need to know God's love and the acceptance of the Christian community.

Hearing Impairment

Hearing impairment may range from mild to complete deafness. Speech and language disabilities often accompany the hearing loss. Learning through "seeing" will be the key to understanding. Visual aids, as well as lip reading and signing, will help to communicate ideas.

Use simple language and talk directly to a child with hearing difficulties. A short, direct statement is best when explaining new words, a story, or an idea in a visual presentation. Be sure your face is in full view of the child. It is not necessary to shout or to exaggerate movements of the mouth.

In one church school, a young adult who knew sign language was asked to be a part of the teaching team. She not only interpreted ideas for a deaf child, but also she taught a small group of children to read and use sign language.

Blind or Partially Blind

Blind or partially blind children develop their other senses to compensate for the lack of vision. In the church school, as in other situations, they learn best by experiencing an idea or concept through feeling, hearing, tasting, and smelling. For use with these children, choose materials for art activities such as wood, cloth, and clay, which are good for touching and feeling. Blind children can take part in discussions or dramatizations by using puppets. It is also helpful for them to listen to recordings or tapes. Older children or youth could make tapes of the material the other children will be reading. For children who have learned to read Braille, Bibles in Braille are available through the American Bible Society.

Mental Disabilities

Children with mental disabilities are often not able to socialize with children of their chronological age. They cannot grasp the ideas that come easily to others. They have short attention spans. They frequently are moving a foot or an arm and are easily distracted. Each child is different.

There are several ways we can help the child with mental disabilities have an easier time within a class of normal students. It is important to provide a structure for the child so he or she knows what is expected and what the limits are. Changes in routines are disturbing to these children. It is best to have one adult who works with a child on a one-to-one basis. The adult may help the child know what is expected of her or him and provide a firm, consistent control for the child. Plan to use activities that are less demanding and on a grade level where the child is functioning. Find out from the parents what the child can do best.

Emotional Difficulties

Jim enters the room with a scream and starts knocking over chairs. Because he is an emotionally disturbed child, the causes and effects of his behavior are many. His learning ability is not usually different from the others, but he will function well only when he discovers friendship and trust in the teacher and the group. Such a child needs one teacher with whom to relate in a special way. This teacher's task is to love and accept the child no matter what he or she does. On days when the child is having a "rough time," this adult needs to give sole attention in a quiet spot. Here the two may talk or work quietly on an activity. This child requires much assurance, affection, affirmation, and firmness.

The Gifted Child

Peter's ability may be considered a handicap as he often faces the misunderstanding of teachers and others in his peer group. As a gifted child, Peter's mental age is much higher than his chronological age. He learns faster, remembers more, and tends to think more deeply about what he learns. Often in the middle of a discussion, Peter takes off on a tangential interest—which makes sense to him but to no one else in the group.

Gifted children may seem shy, obnoxious, or antisocial. They need to be encouraged to think for themselves. A common characteristic of a gifted child is to conform in order to be accepted, rather than give an idea that is different. The gifted child's abilities can be put to work to enrich learning activities in the church school. A younger child may tell about a story he or she has read or share a hobby. An older child may be given some research to do. Care needs to be taken in guiding gifted children to respect others who do not think or learn in the same way as they do. Contrary to what we might think, gifted children need to find self-esteem.

The "special" child needs to have a satisfying feeling of belonging and contributing to the group. A teacher's attitude sets the tone for how other children respond to a "special child." When you show acceptance, respect, expectation, and patience for the person who needs extra consideration, the boys and girls are apt to follow your example. Avoid placing the child in circumstances where the "difference" is obvious. At such times, it is easy for the others to make fun of or feel superior to the child. It may be necessary to find a time—when the special child is not present—to discuss the differences openly and find ways the children may show their under-standing. Children need to know how painful teasing can be. Then they may begin to help each other grow.

Additional leadership is necessary as we include children with special needs in the regular activities of the church. Team teaching, parent volunteers, or assistance from young people can facilitate a teaching-learning situation in which each child has a chance to know God's love.

Children Are Teachers, Too!

Children who are free to bring who they are and what they know to a group share in the teaching-learning experience. In effect, they, too, are teachers.

Children have a natural curiosity and sense of adventure. Teachers may be led by children to explore questions they ask or try their suggestions for a "new way" to do an activity.

Children also have an uncanny way of zeroing right through a complex problem to the simple truth of the matter. Adults will struggle with how to help children relate the meaning of a Bible story to their lives, and then, behold, a child will do the task in a very clear, direct way. Listening to children becomes important as teacher and learner discover meaning together.

Children today have a lot of information. They sometimes do not know what to do with all they know. One teacher thought as he looked over his class, "You know more than I will ever know, but I think I can help you understand what you know."

Teachers who are open to children will learn from them, take what they share, use it, and grow in their own understanding of the Christian faith.

7

Teachers and Teaching

The Role of the Teacher

—as an enabler of learning

Your role as teacher is primarily that of inviting children to share with you in learning. The teacher is responsible for preparing for a session with appropriate objectives for a group of children. The teacher is not *the* authority or power figure. In our ministry with children we like to think of the teacher as an "enabler"—one who helps children to do their own learning. The role of the teacher-enabler is:

- to stimulate the interest of the children.
- to be a resource person who suggests meaningful activities for learning.
- to be a guide in helping children to think through the meaning of biblical material, play experiences, and relationships.
- to help create a community feeling among the children so that they might feel free to express themselves, ask questions, and take the initiative in finding out about the Christian faith.

—as a model in terms of attitudes and behavior

What do children learn from what the teacher says and does? Children first size up a teacher from a self-centered view: "Does he like me?" "Does she think my ideas are good?" A teacher's own expression of love, understanding, and forgiveness of children is readily caught. The teacher's first task is to communicate God's love.

Children next see the teacher as one who is phony or real. They quickly sense when a person is not what he or she pretends to be. Children enjoy a real person for a teacher—one who is a friend and shows interest in them. Yes, they can even respect a person who gets angry and seems a bit bored at times. But how they do enjoy sharing humor and fun with teachers! The teacher who is big enough to admit "I blew it!" "I made a mistake!" is helping children know it's okay to make mistakes. Mistakes can be corrected and forgiven in oneself and in others.

A teacher's attitude may be: "This is the way it is. I know!" or "I'm here because I need to learn and grow with you!" The second attitude helps children to know that one can continue to learn all through life and that God is active in the experience of learning. Children learn many things in quiet, unexpected ways. The teacher is an important model for the growing child.

—as a communicator of values

Children learn values from the important "key" people in their lives. At a young age they become aware that people differ in what they think is "right" and "wrong." A little child is told "No!" while she or he watches another child do the same thing and get away with it.

Television viewing exposes children to a variety of life-styles and values in our pluralistic society. Older children do wonder: *What is right? What is wrong? How can I make a decision?*

You as a teacher communicate values that are important in the Christian community. One way to teach values is to demonstrate them through the learning activities. Children are learning values when they are planning, sharing, looking for meaning, and doing things for others. Such activities can say that human life has value, that persons are different, have rights, and deserve respect.

The Christian church "lives out" the values it stands for in the activities of the church fellowship. You can help the boys and girls understand the reason for the activities and the values they represent. Better still, find ways for them to participate in the activities. Children may see the fellowship, caring, and supporting, believing that life is a gift from God, believing that life is worth living, believing that there is hope for a better life, and worshiping God through prayer and rituals.

Sharing your own convictions is important: "This is what I believe. . . ." "From my experience. . . ." "The way I see things now. . . ." "This is why. . . ." Sharing one's point of view must not mean *imposing* values on children. Share in such a way as to encourage learners to make their own commitment to Christian values.

The Team—or Working Alone!

When teaching with a team, each person shares in guiding the total learning experience in each session. Each team member is a teacher. Each one is aware of what might happen at every point of the session from beginning to end. The team together is ready to give guidance in activities as the session moves along.

A team prepares by planning, studying, praying, and evaluating together. Each person is encouraged to use his or her special abilities

in teaching. Planning involves deciding who will be responsible for the different activities. A team teacher may be assigned a small group activity or a learning center. That person will then prepare for the activity by gathering necessary materials and information. Some teaching teams find it wise to choose a lead teacher for each session. This "key" person is responsible for getting the session started, making transitions, and guiding the children when they are together in a group.

Many teachers find the team approach makes it easier for them to relate to children on a one-to-one basis. Particularly in a large group, children with special needs can be reached when there is more than one teacher. It is also easier to encourage children in their relationships with one another. Because of the possibilities for a variety of groupings and activities, there is often a more informal atmosphere with team teaching. Team teachers also model, through their working together, a relationship based on respect and Christian love.

Teaching alone also works! The teacher working alone will adapt plans and materials to suit the size of the group. The lone teacher will also think realistically about the abilities he or she has to carry out a plan.

A teacher is never alone, however. Children and teacher can be a team. Very young children can become helpers in putting things away. As children grow older, they may share in planning, setting up the interest centers, finding resources, and carrying out separate group projects. It helps to make a chart listing the responsibilities when tasks are shared with children. Allow children to choose what they would like to do. Provide for frequent changes. Older children often work well in small groups or committees. They may be able to plan what they will do and how they will do it with just a little guidance from the teacher. One of the children can be chosen as chairperson. He or she will get the group organized and working on its task, and then report the progress being made by the group.

Whether teaching alone or as a team, it is more satisfying to share the responsibility with others.

A Relationship with the Home

The home is a major influence in a child's life. In our fast-changing world there are a variety of home situations: a traditional nuclear family, a single parent family, an extended family with relatives and/or friends, a group home or institution, a foster home, or a flexible group with people moving in and out.

What children experience in their homes also varies. They may share with the family in talking over problems and in working together. They may seldom see their parents or other members of the family. They may come from a one-child family or they may have brothers and/or sisters. They may suffer physical and/or emotional abuse. They may go on trips which widen their experience or have other privileges which help them to know about the world.

The child's experience in the home affects how he or she learns in the church. The teacher needs to know about each child's home situation.

Keep in Touch

1. Make a personal call in the home to get acquainted with family members.
2. Make phone calls to let those at home know you are interested in them and in the child's Christian growth.
3. Send letters home to give information about learning activities, special projects, family events, parent meetings.
4. When a child is absent, follow up with any of the ways mentioned

above. Alert the pastor immediately if you hear about a family member who has a serious illness or when there is a crisis.

5. Find ways to encourage parents or other adults in the family to guide the child's Christian growth.

6. Send home the parent pieces from the curriculum you are using.

7. Plan study groups in areas such as parenting, children and Christian growth, and Bible study.

8. Enlist family members in learning activities when you need extra help, when they might assist in a particular project, and when they have information or skills to share which fit into your theme of study.

Continuing to Grow

Teaching children is time consuming and demanding. A teacher soon senses the need to grow as a Christian and to renew a sense of perspective. Growth for adults, as for children, is a continuing process. Growing is personal. Growing is enabled by sharing experiences with others.

We who work with children need from time to time to stop and look at ourselves and ask: *What have I learned? What do I want to become? What growth goals would be good for me right now?* Take some time to think about your own needs for growth. Jot down a list of your ideas. Choose one or two realistic goals.

Teachers become learners when they study child development, learn how to plan and guide learning activities more effectively, study the Bible, talk over theological ideas with others, or participate in denominational or ecumenical teacher-training events.

Teachers, like children, learn through questioning, searching, discovering and working with new ideas. Teachers, like children, are learners!

8

Teachers and Planning

Planning is the key to effective teaching. Planning provides a framework and direction for teaching. A teacher with a plan used as a guide can move from it when the situation demands a change.

Planning a Session

Let's look at some practical steps to help you plan a session.

Step 1. Know the direction

Curriculum materials provide this direction for most of us. Skim through the material to get a sweeping overview of the entire course. Statements of purpose are provided in the curriculum. You will notice that sessions are organized into units or clusters. Each unit or cluster has a specific purpose which fits into the overall theme. If you do not use curriculum materials, think through the theme around which you will plan activities.

Step 2. Bring together information

• *About the children*

What are their needs? Interests? Resources?

What kind of experiences do they have which will help them find a personal meaning in this session? Think about individuals. What happened in the last session? What questions were asked that still need to be answered? What activity was left unfinished?

• *About the teachers*

What skills, strengths, and experiences do you have that will enrich this session? What resources do the other teachers have?

• *About the teaching situation*

What kind of space do you have? Is there enough room for the learning activities? What kind of equipment and materials do you have with which to work?

Step 3. Check your information

Look at the information you have gathered. What does it tell you? What does it mean? How do you need to adapt the suggestions to fit the needs and resources of the children and the teachers? Is it possible to find additional space in another room or in a hall to carry out some of the activities?

Step 4. State an objective for the session

An objective is a statement of what a child may learn in a session, rather than what the teacher will do. For example: "The child will know God as one who seeks change in people, and who can be counted on to forgive and love him or her." Many teachers find it helpful to set down *specific* objectives for each session. These are written in terms of what the child will be able to know or do by the end of a session. Here are examples of specific objectives for one fifth grade class:

Find the biblical account of Jeremiah's speech at the temple.

Describe what God expected of people.

Define the word "covenant" in its biblical meaning.

Identify ways people live according to God's covenant.

Objectives help to guide the selection and sequence of activities that go into a session plan.

Step 5. Make a plan

1. Think through learning activities you will use. Are they realistic as you consider the children, the time, the room, and the equipment? How will they help the children apply meaning to their lives?

2. Plan when you will do each activity. Look at the Sample Session Planning Sheet. What activities can be used at the beginning of the session to interest the children? What activities are best when all children are together, work in small groups, or work alone? How will you involve children in evaluating? How can you close a session?

3. Consider the details. Who will be responsible for each activity? How long will it take? Where will you do it? What materials will be needed?

Step 6. Carry out the plan

Be flexible enough to allow for children's ideas and spontaneous kinds of learnings.

Sample Session Planning Sheet

Unit Purpose

Session Objective(s)

What We Will Do	Time Needed	Who Is Responsible	Materials Needed
Room Arrangement (What will make it attractive, practical for activities, interesting?)			
As Children Arrive (The session begins with the arrival of the first child.)			
Session Development Group together Small groups Interest groups (Use of play, conversation, discussion, creative activities, music, audiovisuals.)			
Closing Moments (A time for sharing, summarizing, evaluating, worship, planning ahead.)			
Evaluating			

Step 7. Evaluation

Teachers and children alike need to evaluate. Children may evaluate at the end of a session by talking over: *What did we like best? What did we learn? What questions do we have? What suggestions do we have?* At the end of a unit, evaluation may involve summarizing what was learned in the previous sessions.

The teacher's evaluation will focus on objectives chosen for the session. What happened to indicate the extent to which objectives were reached?

Careful planning insures a good feeling for the teacher and children. Teachers may be more realistic in what they expect. Children are quick to respond when they sense there is a purpose for their gathering and there are exciting things to do.

Using Resources in Planning

Curriculum resources are graded to enable the best teaching-learning experience. The materials often include books for children, resource books with session plans for teachers, and other aids, such as pictures, maps, charts. They are planned for a broad audience and so require local adaptation. Curriculum resources may be ordered from denominational publishing houses.

People have rich resources to share. Look around in your own church and community for people who have traveled, do community social work, or have experience in church missions. It is more exciting to hear persons tell about their own experiences than to read about them. People who have special gifts and hobbies might help with special projects. Senior citizens might tell about your church's history. Their presence will also help children appreciate another generation. You could also invite a church leader to join your class in order to help the children learn about how the church and its people work.

There are many printed resources which help to enrich learning activities. Some of these are: different Bible translations, Bible atlases, Bible dictionaries, maps, posters, and children's books about typical life situations.

Audiovisuals—filmstrips, films, slides, records, tapes, flat pictures—help to clarify meaning and add interest in a session. Curriculum materials often suggest specific audiovisuals to use in a session. School district audiovisual libraries and public libraries are good sources for materials to use with children. Other possible sources include denominational offices, ecumenical centers, and neighboring churches.

Selecting Resource Materials

The first thing to look for in choosing supplementary materials is whether they are designed to help the children you teach to learn and grow in the Christian faith. Do the materials take into consideration how children learn at that age level? Are the materials attractive? Would they be appealing from a child's point of view? Are the pictures colorful and free from too much detail or symbolism? Will they last under hard use by children? When choosing books for children, look carefully at the readability level. Are they written for the reading level and experience of the children with whom you are working? Is the type large enough?

When selecting curriculum materials for elementary children, ascertain how the child will use the material. Does it encourage thinking, the use of creative activities, and does it offer a variety of suggestions so the child has a choice? When choosing teacher's resources, see how many different ways to teach are suggested. What kind of biblical and theological help is provided? What kinds of directions or practical help are included?

Adapting Resources

Not all curriculum resources will fit every person or situation. They are intended as guides. One group of children may work more slowly or faster than another group. With older children there may be a need to expand plans for a session into several sessions to include more activity so that interviews, field trips, and panel discussions may enhance the learning. The amount of time for a session will determine how much of the material it is possible to use. It is more important to remain flexible to meet the needs of the boys and girls than to cover all of the material suggested for each session.

Caring for the Details

Accurate records are essential for our ministry with children. Complete information about every child should be recorded (home address, phone, parents, church affiliation, age, grade in school, name of school, etc.)

This basic information can be obtained when the child is first enrolled. It needs to become a part of a permanent record. Teachers will then make changes in the record as it is necessary. When children come to church alone, someone needs to make contact with the home.

Each teacher will want to keep a separate record which includes, in addition to the basic information, personal notes regarding the child's interests, abilities, and problems. This information may help the teacher to understand the child better. It is for private use only.

Individual attendance records are also important. It is not enough to count heads for the total church school attendance. When a child is absent, we will want to find out the reason. This will help us to be aware of illness or other problems. Showing our concern and interest is important to our ministry with the whole child.

The manner of offering gifts of money differs with each situation. In many churches children have envelopes to place in the church class offering or in the congregational worship service. Children in other churches drop coins in a basket on the table in their room. Whatever your pattern, help the children know what they are doing and why. Children too young to understand the concept of "offering" may think they have to pay for being in the church. Guide the children in understanding how the money will be used to do the work of the church. It is good to have a special time to call attention to the offering by singing or saying a prayer of thanks. In this way, the act of offering may come to mean responding to God with thanksgiving.

Now, It Is up to YOU!

The ideas in this book have been shared to help you in your ministry. In no way are these ideas the last word. There is so much more to discover about children, about ourselves, and about the ways we can be more effective in our ministry. A structure for teaching has not been set for you to follow. The ingredients have been suggested. What happens in your own teaching-learning situation depends on what you and others do.

Glance again through these chapters. With pencil in hand, let the ideas stimulate you to think and dream. What might you do? Let your imaginings lead you to set some long-range goals toward which to work. You may discover there are some ideas you can work with right away! We hope that your study and imaginings will make clear to you the ways your ministry is unique!

Yes, you have a special task! It is up to you to find ways to allow each child with whom you work the freedom to grow in awareness of God and in response to God.

Resources

On Working with Early Elementary Children

Allstrom, Elizabeth, *You Can Teach Creatively*. Nashville: Abingdon Press, 1970. Excellent resource with tips and guidance in providing learning activities which stimulate creativity in children.

Dotts, M. Franklin, and Maryann J., *Clues to Creativity*. New York: Friendship Press, 1974, 1975, 1976. Three volumes, well illustrated, with clear directions on learning activities arranged alphabetically.

Forte, Imogene, and MacKenzie, Joy, *Nooks, Crannies and Corners: Learning Centers for Creative Classrooms*. Nashville: Incentive Publications, 1973. Creative ideas for learning centers.

Furnish, Dorothy J., *Exploring the Bible with Children*. Nashville: Abingdon Press, 1975. Some descriptions and suggestions of how to use the Bible.

Primary School Portfolio, Association for Childhood Education International, 3615 Wisconsin Avenue, NW, Washington, DC 20016. A group of twelve leaflets with such topics as discipline, children's thinking, creative experiences.

Riessman, Frank, *The Inner City Child*. New York: Harper & Row, Publishers, copyright by the author, 1976. The book provides a true picture of inner-city children, pointing out the strengths they gain through their experience.

Tobey, Kathrene M., *Learning and Teaching Through the Senses*. Philadelphia: The Westminster Press, 1970. Why and how to be deliberate about using the senses to enhance learning.

Tompkins, William, *Indian Sign Language*. New York: Dover Publications, 1969. Well-illustrated book of Indian sign language and pictography, descriptions of Indian customs and ceremonies; suggestions of ways the material can be used in learning activities.

Using Learning Centers in Church Education. Design # 1: Designs for Children's Ministry, JED, 1973. Helpful pamphlet that gives directions and specific examples of how to adapt materials for the learning-center approach.

Widber, Mildred C., and Ritenour, Scott T., *Focus: Building for Christian Education*. Philadelphia: United Church Press, 1969. Several chapters dealing with room arrangement and equipment for children. Describes ideal situation.

General

Christian Education and Hearing Impaired Children: A Few Suggestions for Work with Eight to Twelve-Year Olds. New York: Education for Christian Life and Mission, National Council of Churches, Room 708, 476 Riverside Drive, New York, NY 10027. A packet of materials.

Duckert, Mary, *Help! I'm a Sunday School Teacher*. Philadelphia: The Westminster Press, 1969. A practical how-to-do-it approach to teaching in the church school.

Duska, Ronald, and Whelan, Mariellen, *Moral Development: A Guide to Piaget and Kohlberg*. New York: Paulist Press, 1975. Explains stages in the moral development of children in a readable and understandable way.

Geyer, Nancy B., and Noll, Shirley, *Session Planning for Church School Teachers*. Valley Forge: Judson Press, 1971. Moves the reader through a step-by-step approach to session planning.

Gleason, John J., Jr., *Growing up to God: Eight Steps in Religious Development*. Nashville: Abingdon Press, 1975. Describes theological issues he thinks are dealt with as persons grow up.

Isham, Linda, *On Behalf of Children*. Valley Forge: Judson Press, 1975. A perspective on the needs and resources of children which may shape our ministry with children.

Laymon, Charles M., ed., *Interpreter's One-Volume Commentary on the Bible*. Nashville, Abingdon Press, 1971. Provides maps, photographs, drawings, commentary, and help on chronology.

Martin, C. Lewis, and Travis, John T., *Exceptional Children: A Special Ministry*. Valley Forge: Judson Press, 1968. Practical suggestions for teaching methods to use with handicapped persons.

Rood, Wayne, R., *On Nurturing Christians*. Nashville: Abingdon Press, 1972. Helps teachers reflect on their faith and ways their faith can be effectively shared.

Westerhoff, III, John H., *Will Our Children Have Faith?* New York: The Seabury Press, Inc., 1976. Chapter 4 offers a look at how persons grow in the Christian faith.

Index